Whales of the World

Animated Kids Book

Billy Grinslott & Kinsey Marie Books

ISBN - 9781965098363

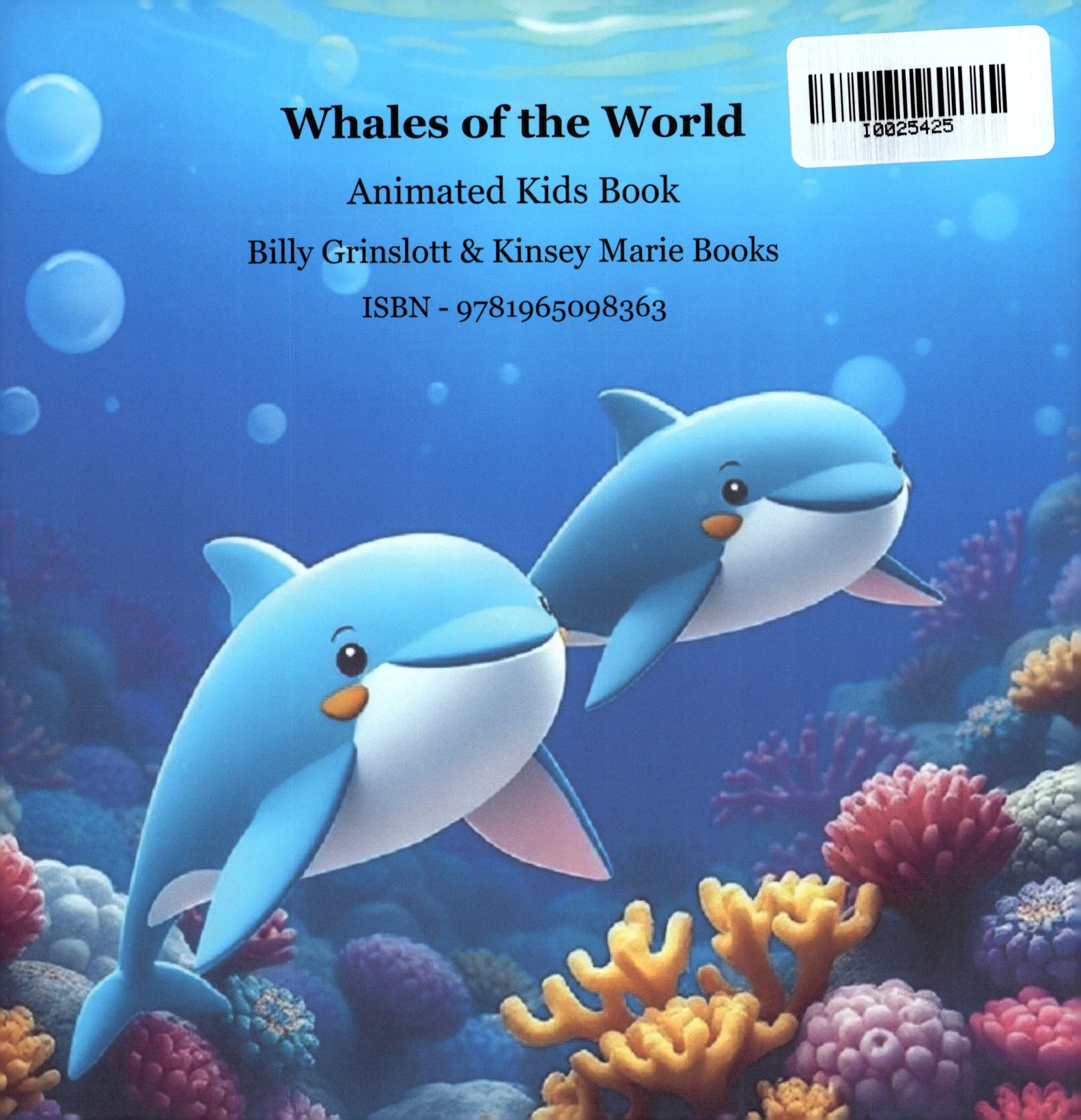

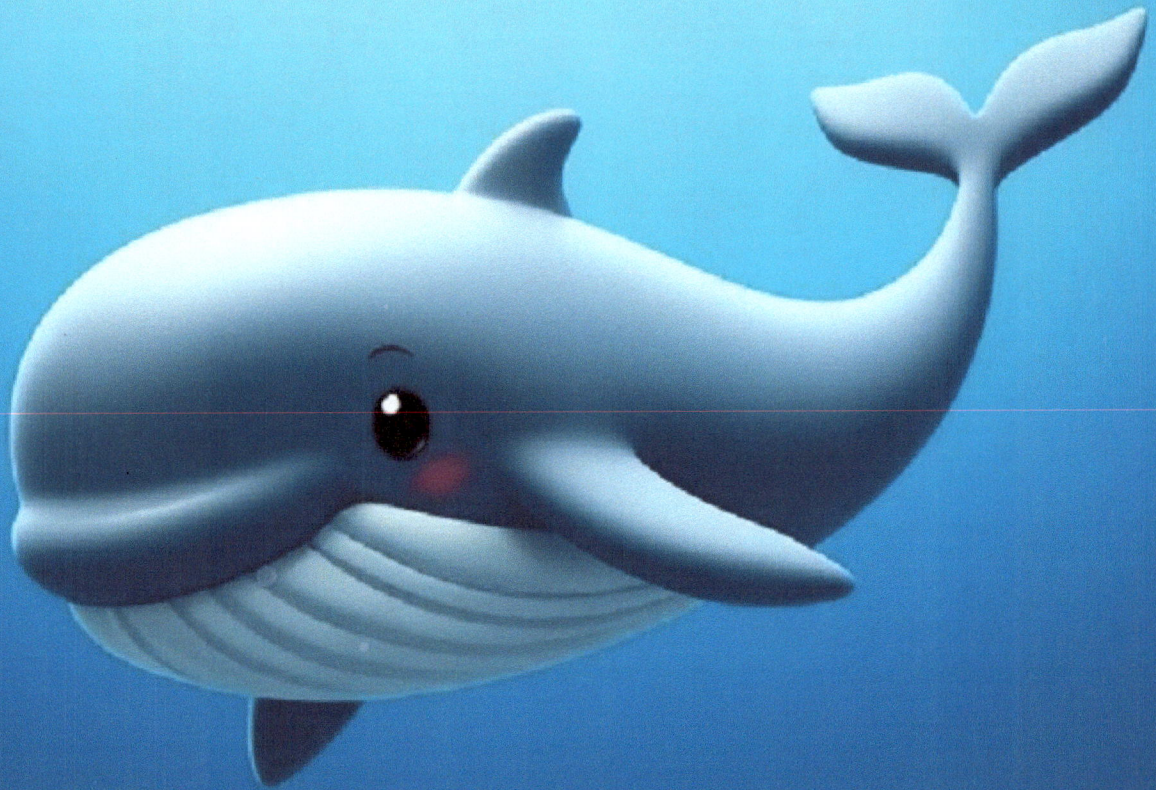

Bowhead Whales can grow up to 60 feet long while still being able to leap entirely out of water. Bowhead whales may be among the longest living animals on earth. They can live to be 200 years old. Bowhead whales have the thickest blubber, layer of fat, of all the whales. Bowhead whales are the only whales to live exclusively in the Arctic.

Pilot whales are long, slender, and relatively small whales from the dolphin family. The pilot whales are very intelligent. Many aquariums and zoos train them to perform for visitors. Pilot whales are very social animals and stay in groups. Pilot whales got their name because it was once believed that each observed group was navigated by a pilot or leader.

Melon headed whales make fast, low leaps from the water as they swim. They like to rest in the morning, socialize in the afternoon, and feed at night. They are named for their small heads with large melons, oil-filled foreheads that allow them to see with sound waves. These whales are very social, they live in large groups numbering between 100 and 1,000.

The narwhal has a long tusk on its face. Their tusk can grow as long as ten feet. They spend their lives in the cold Arctic waters and change color with age. They can dive as deep as 4,500 ft. Narwhal whales can spend more than three hours a day underwater, before coming up for air. They use their tusks for spearing fish and breaking ice.

Pygmy right whales have a small head compared to their body size. Unlike right whales, pygmy right whales have sleeker, more streamlined bodies that are topped with a small, sickle-shaped dorsal fin. This whale can be found living in the Southern Ocean and is considered the smallest of the baleen whales.

Northern and Southern Right Whales. Right whales grow up to 52 feet long and weigh up to 63 tons. North Atlantic right whales are one of the world's largest whales. Remarkably, because they only eat zooplankton like copepods and krill larvae. There are fewer than 360 of these whales left on Earth.

Gray whales play an important role in the Arctic Ocean due to their unique style of bottom-feeding. They create gigantic mud plumes that raise large volumes of nutrients into the water that other fish can eat. Gray whales reach 40-50 feet in length and can weigh as much as 40 tons.

Bowhead Whales can grow up to 60 feet long while still being able to leap entirely out of water. Bowhead whales may be among the longest living animals on earth. They can live to be 200 years old. Bowhead whales have the thickest blubber, layer of fat, of all the whales. Bowhead whales are the only whales to live exclusively in the Arctic.

Fin whales can grow up to 85 feet long and weigh 72 tons. Fin whales can live up to 90 years. Fin whales have accordion-like throats that help them gulp up to 4,000 pounds of food a day. Fin whales are fast swimmers and are known to raise their heads above the water, while swimming. It is found throughout the world's oceans.

Baleen whales include twelve different species of marine mammals, including humpbacks and gray whales. Their name comes from the baleen plates that are used to trap food by straining ocean water. They can hear and communicate with each other under water. They can grow to 180 tons.

There are two species of Bryde's whales. The Eden's whale is a smaller form found in the Indian and western Pacific oceans. The Bryde's whale is named after a Norwegian man called Johan Bryde who discovered the species. Bryde's whales spend most of the day within 50 feet of the water's surface. They commonly swim at 4 miles per hour but can reach speeds of 15 miles per hour. They can dive to depths of 1,000 feet.

Balaenoptera whales body is more streamlined, the snout is more pointed or rounded. There are eight different species of whale in this group. They grow to a length of 100 feet and weigh up to 200 tons. They are found in all oceans except the Arctic. They generally migrate seasonally between feeding grounds.

Omura's whale is the most recently identified whale species. They were first recognized in the wild in 2015. So far, they have been spotted in all oceans except the central and eastern Pacific. Omura's whales are seen off Madagascar all year round. Omura's whale is one of the smallest whales within the baleen whale group, only growing to about 33 feet in length.

First recognized in the Gulf of Mexico in 1965. In 2021, the Rice's whale was recorded as its own new species. Rice's whale is the only year-round resident baleen whale in the northern Gulf of Mexico. At an estimated population size of only 51 animals, it is one of the world's most endangered baleen whales.

The sei whale is one of the fastest whales, reaching speeds of up to 35 miles per hour. Sei whales inhabit all oceans and adjoining seas except in tropical and polar regions. Sei whales dive differently than most whales. They do not arch their backs or show their flukes before diving, they simply sink below the surface. Sei whales are the 3rd largest whale.

False killer whales can dive for up to 18 minutes and swim at high speeds to catch fish at depths of 1600 feet. They often leap completely out of the water. In Hawaii, they are also known to throw fish high into the air before eating them. False killer whales are members of the dolphin family. They generally live in deep, offshore tropical, and sub-tropical waters.

Beaked whales got their name because they have a long snout. Beaked whales hold the record for the deepest and longest dive for any mammal. Beaked whales are a cetacean family that includes 21 species. Despite being the second largest family, they are one of the least known.

Bottlenose whales are one of the few whales that have a snout. They get their name because their snout resembles a bottle. Bottlenose Whales are one of the deepest-diving mammals known, able to dive as deep as 4700 feet. They prefer deep waters and rarely venture into areas that are shallower than 2500 feet.

Pygmy Killer Whale are generally less active than other whales and are frequently seen resting in groups at the surface oriented the same way or direction. Pygmy killer whales are very aggressive and do not do well in captivity. The Pygmy killer whale only grows to 400 pounds when fully mature.

The dwarf sperm whale is a small whale, about 8 feet in length and around 600 pounds. Dwarf sperm whales are very similar to the pygmy sperm whale. The dwarf sperm whale inhabits temperate and tropical oceans worldwide, in particular continental shelves and slopes.

Sperm whales are the largest of all toothed whales and can grow to a maximum length of 52 feet and weight of 90,000 pounds. Sperm whales have the largest brain of any living animal, weighing up to 9 pounds. The longest recorded dive for a sperm whale was more than 2 hours long.

Toothed Whales are a group of whales that have actual rounded teeth, compared to baleen whales that have short, stubbed teeth. Some of the toothed whales are, the sperm whale, the dwarf and pygmy sperm whale, the beluga whale, the narwhal, and the beaked whales. There are 77 species of toothed whales.

Minke whales are the smallest of the great whales, growing to about 35 feet long and weighing up to 20,000 pounds. Minke whales can stay submerged for at least 15 minutes before returning to the surface for air. Minke whales live up to 50 years. Minke whales are the most common of the great whale species and can be found throughout the world's oceans.

Humpback whales grow up to 60 feet long and weigh 80,000 pounds. Humpback whales can live for 90 years. Humpback whales have some of the longest migrations of any mammal with some swimming 5,000 miles. Humpback whales eat up to 3,000 pounds of food a day. Humpback whales create and sing songs that can be heard up to 20 miles away. Humpback whales are named for the distinctive hump on their backs.

Orcas, known as killer whales, are the largest member of the dolphin family. A male orca can be 32 feet in length and weigh 22 thousand pounds, as big as a school bus. Orcas are intelligent and able to coordinate maneuvers. Orcas are extremely fast swimmers. Orcas live in every ocean in the world. They sleep with one eye open and can see any other fish coming their way.

The beluga whale is easily recognizable thanks to its stark white coloring and globular head. Belugas are very social animals, and it's possible to see pods numbering in the hundreds. Beluga whales are one of the most vocal of all whales. These white whales are born dark gray. It can take up to eight years before they turn completely white. The beluga can change the shape of its forehead, by blowing air around its sinuses.

Blue whales are the largest animals ever known to have lived on Earth. These awesome whales rule the oceans at up to 100 feet long and upwards of 200 tons. Blue whale babies are the biggest on Earth. At birth they weigh around 8,800 pounds, with a length of 26 feet. Fully grown they can weigh as much as 30 elephants.

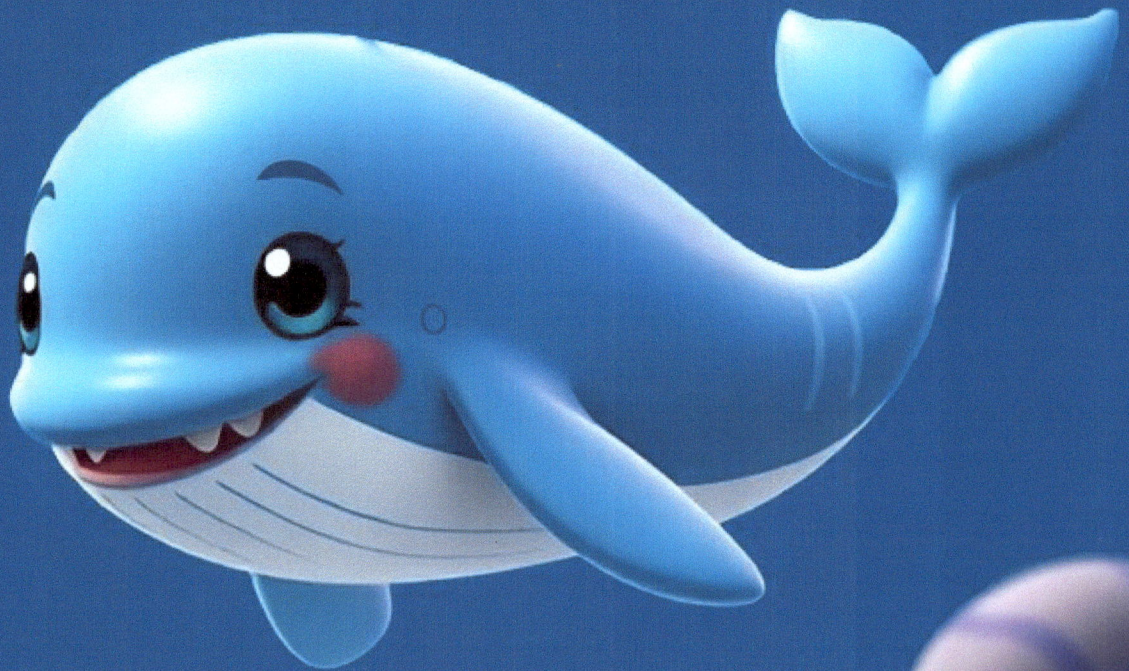

Fun Facts About Whales

Blue whales are the largest animals to have ever lived on Earth.

Sperm whales have the largest brain of any animal on Earth.

Blue whales appear blue because of thousands of tiny algae on their skin.

Sperm whales sleep standing up, with their tails dangling downwards.

Whales sing for a variety of reasons, including to communicate, find a partner, or keep an eye on their young.

Captive whales have been known to mimic human speech.

There are types of whales: baleen whales and toothed whales.

Whales breathe air through blowholes on the top of their heads.

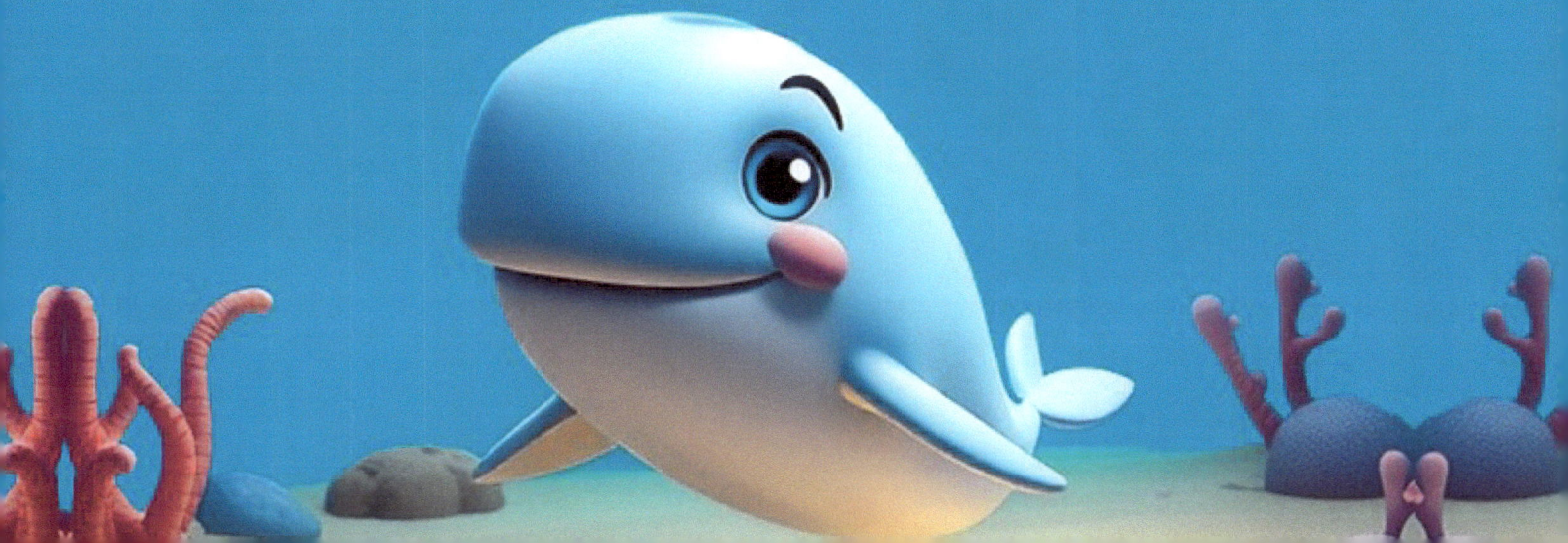

Author Page

Billy Grinslott & Kinsey Marie Books

ISBN – 9781965098363

Thanks